Abnormal Behavior

Personal Experiences

"While all forms of thinking should be tolerated, some forms of behavior should not be. In the end it is behavior that counts."

From *A Different Drum* by M. Scott Peck, MD

To
   DANIEL MEENdo
      BEST WISHES

From

   Charles R. Lambert, SR

Abnormal Behavior

Personal Experiences

Charles R. Lambert, Sr.

Old Mountain Press

Published by:
Old Mountain Press, Inc.
2542 S. Edgewater Dr.
Fayetteville, NC 28303

www.oldmountainpress.com

Copyright © 2005 Charles R. Lambert, Sr.
Interior text design by Tom Davis
Edited by Dr. Polly B. Davis, Ms. Fredricka Petty Proveaux, and
Bro. Lance Justice
ISBN: 1-931575-63-0
Library of Congress Control Number: 2006902346

Abnormal Behavior: Personal Experiences.

First Edition
Printed and bound in the United States of America by Morris
Publishing • www.morrispublishing.com • 800-650-7888
1 2 3 4 5 6 7 8 9 10

I dedicate this work to the men and women of
Mental Health,
My wife,
Judy Burris Lambert,
My son,
Charles R. Lambert, Jr.,
And
THE BROTHERHOOD

Acknowledgments

I just have to mention some folks who helped me along the way: my neighbor and friend, Ms. Freddie Proveaux, who edited for me and guided me; Ms. Elizabeth Lister, a church buddy, friend, and helper; Lance Justice, also a church buddy; my latest friend, COL (Ret) Tom Davis of Old Mountain Press, who typeset this work and provided valuable assistance; my last Editor, Dr. Polly Davis; Morris Publishing for designing my book cover and excellent printing of the book; and countless others who work for Mental Health. Thank you one and all.

Charles R. Lambert, Sr.

Foreword

Years and years I have pondered over this piece of literature. I had to decide whom I was trying to reach with this material. I would like for it to sit on the shelves of the Gospel Advocate in Nashville, Tennessee, beside my other book "PINK PENCIL." Therefore I had to clean up my work. I am a warrior and a Paratrooper. And some deeds have been done to me and others that should not be read in Church, nor should be spoken about in the homes of Christians. Nevertheless, Jesus Christ walked and talked among sinners and unbelievers. His ministry was not in church, for the church was established after His death.

A warrior's life is not easy, and certainly not scriptural, yet necessary. Wars are mentioned in the book of Genesis, the first book of the Bible. There will always be wars and people to be trained to fight these wars. It may offend you, but people die in wars. There was no love present when a man thrust a sword into another man's body. Yet afterwards, there may have been feelings of remorse. May God have mercy on all the men and women of valor from Genesis until the end of time.

I pray that this book will help Christians and others understand my life with mental illness. Like war, it is not a pretty picture. I want everyone to understand that behavior can be changed with hard persistent work. Day after day of hard work spend studying yourself and your innermost thoughts can be very rewarding.

I can neither change the world nor some of my behavior. Sometimes I use behavior that I learned in my youth when I have no control over a situation. My anger comes out in profane words when I lose control. This vice persists even after much praying and years of worshiping God. I pray that God will forgive me of my sins each day. And at judgment day I know God loves me enough to let me enter with the saints.

I want men and women to read this book to better understand some realities of my struggles with mental health and a Paratrooper's will to fight everyday of his life for God and country. I want to share my story of fighting mental illness that others may benefit by my experiences. I want the world to know I have experienced the love of Almighty God, a love that has saved my life day after day.

The youth of today will determine whether our country will be a Democracy 100 years from now. It seems to me that today's teens in this country are too involved with unimportant things like crazy music and the in-things to do which are killing our youth's chance to survive. We may be the strongest power on earth, yet our morals are becoming weaker every day. God is still in control of this world, and not Satan. The innocent little child is a lot closer to God, yet we must become as little children if we are to enter the kingdom of God. We also must seek first the kingdom of God and focus only on the most important things of this life. As Jesus said, "Suffer not the little children to come unto me, for such is the kingdom of God."

Brother A.B. Carroll, an evangelist, answered a question put to him by yours truly, "What if there is no heaven"? His simple answer was, "Do you know of a better life than a Christian life?" There is none better than loving one another and taking care of those who can not take care for themselves. It is impossible to sneak anything past God's eyes as they do at the welfare office. The love to carry on day after day is found only when we put God first in our lives. When we raise our families in the church, we have this love for God and for each other and it sustains us everyday of our Christian life.

I pray you will find love for yourself, love for your country, and love for God our maker. I also hope that you will support the fight against mental illness and visit a Veterans Hospital to see the men who laid down their lives for your freedom to worship God.

Charles R. Lambert, Sr.

Contents

Extreme Behavior

Personal Experience

Today folks boast about going to their therapist, psychologist, doctor, or mental health center. It is the thing to do. But just thirty years ago, to be mentally ill was to be a castaway. Why? Mostly because of ignorance or not knowing the truth. I can personally say thirty years ago I did not know what mental illness was, and I certainly was an emotionally disturbed person. I have no problem saying I was crazy for a short time. Had I not received treatment, I could have hurt my wife or son or someone else and regretted it for the rest of my life. I had to be protected from myself and others.

This is the beginning of a book I want to share with the world, for my life is an open book to anyone who wants to intrude or take a stroll with a person who has been mentally ill all of his life. I will tell you what your friends and doctors won't tell a patient. Believe it or not, most of the time it is for the person's best interest. I have been unable to function like the average human most of my life. In the last few years, drugs have been improved, changed, and discovered that have given me a better quality of life than I have ever had before. I am not going to tell you all the thoughts that run through my mind, for I would be put away; nevertheless, we all have thoughts that could put us away.

At the age of ten I realized I was euphoric when my mood swings went out of my control. I had learned at an early age to hate, and it festered and grew in me until I had no love for anybody or anything. I was just tormented inside. What brought this behavior about? I had a dad who was raised during the depression. His mother died at his birth, so he lived with his kinfolks. His father outlived three or more wives, and he had several half brothers and sisters. They tried to make him work for them, and he did, but only when he wanted to. He had a mind of his own. His dad was a watchman at a lumberyard, and sometimes at night he would go look his father up at his job. There he made a bed for himself, spending the night by the only real relative he had left. I recall him saying things were as bad as Hoover's days.

He had no education, but he could sign his name; he signed it Charley, which is the old way of spelling it.

Those years were hard for all of us because Dad could not get a job anywhere except the paper mill. He was a laborer and could go no higher up the pay scale. He provided for his family. He grew up on the farm when that was the only way to make a living. So he always had a large garden, and we had to work in the garden. I hated to get up at daybreak and pick beans. Those years the mosquitoes and yellow flies were terrible, and we had to wear clothing to protect us. We had to put on insect repellent, which was greasy and burned while the sweat ran freely. We all hated the work, but he taught us to work.

The first time he whipped me with a belt I was about four. He did it because I hit him first. I wanted to fight because I did not want to ride on the back of a truck. I tackled his legs and tried to hurt him. He asked me if I was finished, and he took his belt and whipped me with a strap for the first time. There was much more to come. As the years went by, there were more lashings. He made it known when he came into the house the kids had better find a corner to hide in. If we had a visitor, we had to sit and be very quiet. There was nothing wrong with that except we were all frightened to death. The three oldest children (and I was the oldest) had it a lot harder than the last three children. There were six of us. I was not a very good student in school, and, brother, we walked lightly when report cards came in. I had a learning disability, and although I tried hard to please him by bringing home good grades, I could not come home and do any homework.

It all came to a head when one morning about 4:00 a.m. he came into my bedroom, pulled the covers off me, and whipped me with his special belt made just for me, telling me over and over how much he loved me. While something in me believed him, these beatings taught me what hate really was. In my confusion, I always believed that he was a good man because he never hit or hurt my mother. I still loved him because I believed he always loved her. Before he died, he asked me to take care of her. But he drove me away. Because I hated and feared him, when he died, I rejoiced. I tell you this so that you can understand how his behavior affected my whole life as you will read in the following chapters.

My story is one of sadness and despair, but also of redemption, joy, and love. My sincerest hope is for this book to help others find themselves and have a choice as to the kind of behavior that would satisfy themselves.

Assistant Professional Golfer

One afternoon after school we went exploring among the beautiful green fairways and greens of the new golf course which had been built just a mile or so from my home. We did not know what the game of golf entailed until we walked out onto the 9th fairway and a man put a club into our hands. I guess he just wanted to see how ignorant we were about an instrument called a 3 wood. We tried hitting that little ball over and over, and when we were unable to hit the thing, it amused the men even more. We were chased away, but I found out some very important information. I heard that a kid could make a dollar carrying those clubs in a golf bag for a man when he played golf. I loved the bright green color of everything at the golf course. I also learned the name of the boy that carried the golf clubs for a golfer - caddy.

I decided to become one of these caddies, for one dollar was a lot of money for a few hours of strolling around the golf course. I was one of a few boys who tried to make a dollar after school. I showed up at the golf course every hour I could spend there. The other white boys gave up, and that left me and a lot of colored boys leaning against the wall of the clubhouse waiting to be chosen to carry one of these golf bags. I caddied for some important folks in town. Some were doctors and attorneys, all respected people in the community. I decided right away that I was going to be in the golf business. I did not know how or when or where, but I now had a direction in life.

I hung around, leaning on the wall with the other caddies, until one day the professional asked me to shag some balls for him. He hit them, and I picked them up and put them in this nice little bag until he finished practicing. There was another surprise in store for me: he asked me to take his clubs to the first tee. It was my first round with the professional as his caddie. I knew I just had to become a golfer. In time, I caddied for the professional, Mr. John Watson, each time he played a round of golf. I learned a stipulated round of golf was 18 holes. Two trips around the course was two dollars and a tip. I was rich beyond belief! Caddying was my first real job. Everything at the course was very new and different, and I could not stay away. Another plus was that the people were so nice to me. It sure was better than sitting in a corner afraid to move. I worked my way into the golf shop as assistant professional. Wow! What excitement was ahead of me. I could not believe my good fortune.

Mr. John Watson took me under his wing and gave me a chance. I worked my heart out for him and his wife Lillian. They had two young children, a boy and a girl, who always came by the shop to play. We were all young then, and life was so exciting in the golf business. Mrs. Watson treated me like a son although it was her father, Mr. Fred Thompson, that laid the ground work for some of my best behavior. The behavior that I acquired working for and with him improved my character in ways that I am still proud of today. He was a hard man to do business with; his way was hard but had proven him successful over the years. He told me he once had twenty women working for him, and he fired them all and hired twenty men, whom he also fired. I never understood how he got the work done, but Mr. Thompson did find a way to accomplish his task; it brought about my job as an assistant golf professional.

There were times we joked, but I listened a lot to Mr. Thompson because my dad Charley had taught me respect for my elders. My duties were to empty and wash four trash cans each night and sweep the floors, two locker rooms, and the golf shop. Those were my worst duties. Mr. Thompson always called the golf shop the Golf Club when he answered the telephone. For the rest of the day, I ran the golf shop with Mr. Thompson. I answered the phone the way Mr. Thompson taught me, and I also ran the cash register the way he taught me. I will never forget one of his very important rules, "Everything has its place, and everything will be in its place, always."

Mr. Thompson was from Canada, and he and his wife, whom he nick-named Tiny, only came down for the fall and winter because the summers were too hot for him. He always had a cigar in his mouth or his hands. I watched him take out a new cigar, clip off the end of it with a razor type cutter, place it in his holder (he always used a plastic cigar holder), and light it up. He loved his cigars and even strong drink sometimes. He never yelled at me, but he was firm; and I respected everything he told me. He told me about his days during World War II. I recall how he went into draft dodgers' homes and pulled them out from under the bed, cuffed them, and placed them in the service of their country. He was a tough customer; yet he had a gentle side, and we loved each other's company. He gave me a great honor before I saw him the last time: he gave me a Second World War bayonet that he had taken off a dead German during the war. I treated him like my own father, and, in return, he treated me like a son. He told me when he died he would be cremated and his ashes would rest on the mantel of his home.

John Watson was about the only man I called by his first name. It was unusual, but we were both comfortable with first name basis. I always called his wife Mrs. Watson. She introduced me to my very first ham and cheese, lettuce and tomato sandwich. John taught me how to refinish wooden golf clubs. After I refinished them, he sold them; we both made a profit. I also had a shoeshine business. I knew what every person's foot smelled like at the club. A quarter or fifty cents in those days was good pocket money.

John Watson and Lillian Watson took me to the Master's Golf Tournament in the year 1958. What a thrill! When I saw all those golfers hitting the ball with such power and precision, I was sure the golf profession was for me. I saw Sam Snead, Ben Hogan, and Arnold Palmer, who won the Masters that year. The morning we traveled to Augusta was rainy, but the tournament went on as scheduled. Sam Snead hit a drive off one of the tee boxes, and Mrs. Watson picked up the tee, for Mr. Snead did not look for a tee after a drive like that. She gave me the tee, which was my first souvenir of the Masters Golf Tournament. It was a wonderful day in my life, and golf had made it possible.

Cruising Coastal South Carolina

In the 11th grade, some things changed that made me make a decision about my life. It was a decision I had to make if I was to have any peace of mind at the age of seventeen. Like everyone else in high school, I was always looking for a place to make money. I had my driver's license by then, and I was cruising when I noticed a funny type of restaurant being built. There was someone working there that evening, so I drove up to the entrance and went inside where I met a guy named Dell Thompson. This man was out of the service and helping his brother-in-law start a new business. We became best friends. I needed someone his age to confide in and look up to. I still worked at the golf course, but I could not confide in John. Dell and I hit it off right away. It seemed like he never met a stranger. I even worked part time for his brother-in-law.

Those were the days. We all grew up on the beaches of South Carolina. We worked all day and partied all night. I helped Dell in the restaurant, and he looked out for me. The other guys that came around were much larger than I was. When Dell went to the beach, he never left me behind. We all believed Dell was a hero, and in a way he was. Some older guys went with us when we all congregated at the Tee Pee Drive Inn Restaurant. We partied all Friday night and got in just in time to open up the restaurant on Saturday morning. Then it was the time to make the onion rings. The drive-in had 180 degree windows, and the sun poured in on us. We sweated all morning, but that night after closing we hit the beach again. That summer we crashed many house parties, and the girls seemed as glad to see us as we were to see them.

We went to a house party of college students one evening. The whole crowd was drunk with beer, and someone started a fight. The men were fighting over the women, their feet bleeding from the broken bottles on the floor. We had some very close calls that night, but I thought it was just part of growing up on the beach.

During this time, my dad was hot on my trail, just waiting for me to do something wrong – or just do anything. Mr. John Watson made an decision that I would work at the golf course and in the club house, which was a great opportunity for me. But I had itchy feet. I was dating two girls at the time. One would have married me, and the other turned me down.

Dell shared stories with us about his time in the Airborne Rangers. I had decided to become a paratrooper a number of years before I met him.. I had to leave, to get away and think. I was cutting the number 9 fairway when I made the decision. So I left the golf course that moment and went home to ask my dad to sign for me to get into the service. I think he was delighted, and we went to see the Army recruiter. It did not take long, and I was on my way to Fort Jackson, S.C., before sundown. Dell's talk about the service, coupled with the world's closing in on me at the time, brought about the decision of my life.

I can remember looking up at the stars as the bus rolled along. There were only a few people on the bus. I was breaking all ties as a kid or teenager, and I knew I could not turn back. I had not even shaved for the first time yet, and I had struck out on my own. I knew there was much more to life than living in my small town and working at a plant or a mill. That was not for me. My dad had no choice as to where he worked, but I was determined to get out of town. I have never regretted leaving; but some tough times lay ahead.

Signing On with Uncle Sam

I arrived at Fort Jackson about eleven o'clock, January 13, 1961. I got off the bus, took my small suitcase in hand, and walked up the steps to a new life. I was smoking Winston cigarettes at the time, and I flipped the cigarette butt into the yard. There were a couple of GIS watching me, and I heard them say loudly, "You will be sorry." I soon found out they knew what they were talking about. I had not eaten anything all evening, and they were nice enough to give me some blankets and sheets and a couple of sandwiches. For many days to come I woke up and went to sleep to a trumpet call. There were guys from all walks of life. Most of them had been drafted and were married with kids. Before I was ever sworn in, I learned firsthand about "hurry up and

31

wait" and what a complaining G.I. sounded like in the Army. They screamed and hollered, and it was serve your time or do jail time. No one knew what would happen next. We were all informed as to what was expected of us. I had volunteered (RA). But if I had answered the draft (US), I could have extended a year and collected $1000.00. But no one told me, and I hadn't asked; this was another lesson I learned in the service.

The recruiter swore I would be able to attend classes in the Army and finish my high school education. In reality, the only education I received in the Army was in the school of "hard knocks." We were sworn in as soldiers for the U.S. Armed Forces; some took tests and were interviewed. We were asked our civilian occupation. I told them about my experiences in golf, and the man said, "Mister, you will have it made, for you will do the same thing in the service." I balked at that and told him I wanted to join the 101st Airborne, Fort Campbell, Kentucky. He asked me to change my mind, but my mind was made up. I wanted to jump from an airplane in flight. He looked me right in the eye and told me, "You are not tall enough, not big enough, and you are not mean enough." That just made me more determined. He said, "They will have to put a cannonball in your pocket so you will come down to earth and not go up with the wind."

I was stationed at Fort Jackson for my basic training. There were some things that I remember well. My platoon leader was a black man. I never went to school with black or colored kids, and that was a shock. But I liked him better than some of the other platoon leaders. He was a fair and good man, also a good soldier. I had K.P. once during basic training and got clipped again. I was so gullible. One of the cooks borrowed the only $5.00 I had to my name, and I never saw him again. Since I had volunteered to go Airborne, the company commander took all who were going to Airborne divisions under his wing. He made us work harder and drill longer than the rest of the company. We had to do more physical training (the Army's daily dozen exercises) and run further than the company ran each day.

I did excel in my training and got on the best side of my company commander and my platoon leader with a real act of heroism. It seems we were about to have a large inspection, one of the millions you have in the service, and something was missing. Someone had confiscated the mirror from the jailhouse wall close to our barracks where the 1st

CHARLES R. LAMBERT, SR.

sergeant and the company commander's offices were located. The mirror was stationed there for recruits to check themselves and their uniforms before entering the orderly room. It was very important to the entire company, especially when it was stolen.

The platoon leader called a meeting of the platoon late one afternoon. The order was: "Don't say, tell, or breathe a word of this, but we have got to have a mirror for the inspection coming up." We paired up and set out to find a mirror for the company orderly room. We searched everywhere even though every orderly room was covered, guarded and waiting for the least suspicious recruit with mirror-snatching on his mind.

I was walking along a street where the stockade or jailhouse was located. I walked slowly by and looked at the barbed wire fence and the bars on the doors with guards posted. Right across the street was the Military Police Station, and they were all having a good old time. But they had a mirror out in front of their orderly room. I walked nonchalantly across the front of the place and saw it was screwed onto the wall. I continued on my way back to the barracks where I commandeered a screwdriver. Returning to the M.P. post with the jailhouse across the street and the M.P.'s having a good old time inside, I took the mirror down with no resistance. Carefully I made my way back to my barracks with the mirror tucked under my arm. The next day the word was out. Someone had confiscated the mirror off the jailhouse wall with the guards standing there looking at him! No one believed it. However, a few days later we were marching down the same street with our company commander. He looked over and saluted me with his right hand. I was honored and pleased I could do my part in the case of the missing mirror. I remember this well today, even that the first joints of his hand were missing. He later told me this was due to frost bite in the Korean conflict. He was one of those silent heroes.

After basic training at Fort Jackson and a few days leave, we reported back to be shipped to Fort Benning, Georgia. There we underwent more training and another eight weeks of hard work, trying to become worthy of the uniform we wore. Our first trip to town taught us a lesson. We met some civilians in a park who were celebrating, like we were. We all took a drink and were soon arrested for possession of alcohol in a state park. There were five or more of us who were carted off to the "tank" or civilian jail. We got there, and the jailer took pity on us. He said to us, "Boys, if you pay a small fine, I will let you return to the Base and you will not have to spend the night in jail." However, there was one "Jack-leg" that started arguing with the jailer about his rights and his innocence. The jailer had no choice but to turn the key on all of us. He took us over to our "quarters" for the evening: a commode out in the open - no privacy, a small sink, and a number of bunks with no covers.

It was in the spring, and I was sure this was the end of the line. Surely the company commander would punish us with a cat-o'-nine-tails. I was worried sick. The bunks in the jail were all full, but one of my buddies, a long, tall man and a good friend, said, "We can share this one, how about it?" That was the most encouraging news I had all that day. We lay down back to back in our khaki uniforms, trying to catch a wink. Daylight came fast, and someone from the company was there to take us home. We were all worried, but no one said a word; nevertheless, we had to appear in court and pay an $8.00 fine. We were so relieved we never left the post again, but the guy that caused us to get locked up in the first place ran away that same day - AWOL.

Airborne!

Basic training and infantry training were necessary before being assigned to an Airborne unit. I chose Fort Campbell and the 101st because I just wanted to see Tennessee and Kentucky. I ended up falling in love with those two states and remained there a number of years after my time in the service. When we arrived at Fort Campbell, all the injured personnel lined up to greet us. Soldiers with sprained ankles, broken legs, and broken arms all stood there calling us "legs." A "leg" was a person who was not a paratrooper. We had to prove we were worthy to wear the wings of a paratrooper.

We started out doing a lot of K.P., or kitchen patrol, until we almost dropped from the long hard hours. When the paratroopers came into the chow hall, they all booed, cursed, and yelled at us "legs." The whole idea was to scare us to death, and they did just that. We had to overcome all obstacles in order to earn and wear a paratrooper's wings.

Jumping out of a perfectly good airplane seems crazy to some people although that was really the easy part of the training. We had work after jump school. The evenings were spent cleaning officers' and enlisted men's office areas, waxing the floors. In fact, we were elected to do any dirty detail that came up. Then we got ready for the next grueling day by hand washing our clothes. The physical training or P.T. could fail you faster than anything.

Overcoming being a "leg" in a company of paratroopers was the hardest thing I have ever done. I wanted to be relieved of this pressure when I realized what I was up against. I just had to get into jump school because the "legs" were not allowed to wear decent starched fatigues like the paratroopers. We had to hand wash our clothes; therefore, we stood out as "legs." Wherever we were, we were on display and hated by the company. The details, the K.P., and possibility of rejection were killing me.

One day I was on a detail that I had not volunteered for, and I got the idea to bribe a sergeant in charge of us "legs." I told him I would give him a fifth of whisky if he would get me into jump school. I got into jump school early like I had planned, but they tried to court marshal the sergeant for accepting a bribe. I would not testify against him because he had done me the largest favor anyone had done for me since entering the service.

It was in the month of June that I took my jump school training. We did P.T., and the sweat ran freely. When it did, they marched us through a line of showers to wet us down. They worked us hard, but they were fair. Giving ten to twenty pushups rewarded any parachute landing fall (PLF) mistake we might have made. When I had to do pushups, I got up smiling, for I knew it was for my own preservation. We did PLF's until we did them perfectly. We practiced exiting a mock aircraft until we got that right. The 50 foot tower was fun. It was a mock aircraft with two exit doors fifty feet off the ground. Each man had a step waiting to move up the tower stairway, which had 6 levels. Upon entering the mock aircraft from the stairwell, two jump masters hooked us up to a harness, which was attached to our dummy parachute harness. We took up the door position when the jump master said "STAND IN THE DOOR" to jump from the mock craft or tower. When that jump master said "GO," we had to jump. The odds were not in our favor though. All our weight pulled the webbing or risers that connected us to a parachute together with a slap against both ears, as we slid down the cable pulley apparatus and landed on the mound at the foot of the cable ride. Then it was our turn to run that riser cable pulley back to the tower for the next jumper. Some of us were running around with bleeding ears if we were poor listeners or trouble makers. That jump master could hold that webbing or risers back until the right moment and "Powell," he got your ears.

While walking up the stairs of the fifty foot tower, I never could get it down exactly right, so when I got to the door and received the command to "Go!," I stopped in the door. The two instructors said, "Lookie here, what do we have here?" I screamed out loud, "I want to do it right." So they said, "Take up the door position" (feet together, head down, both hands on the reserve on my stomach). Then to my surprise, they picked me up and threw me out of the door. It split both ears, but I was happy - Airborne! They gave me a good grade on that exit. It was all hard work, but it was worth every drop of sweat. I was in top physical condition until just about the end of my training. Just before we jumped for the last time, my right knee began swelling, and it was painful, but I tried not to limp. Then came the final day of the training. We had to pass the P.T. test, and the most difficult part was the run all the way around the base. This was no surprise. We had been running every day as part of the training; in fact, we never went anywhere while in training without having to run all the way.

The morning had arrived. If we dropped out on this run, we would be reevaluated, which meant we either went through the class again or dropped out of airborne training. Every instructor was beside his class as we began that five-mile airborne shuffle. The instructors called, "Ain't no use in looking down, Ain't no discharge on the ground. Honey, oh baby, now. Go to your left, to your right, left. Go to your left, right, left." We broke a sweat, and our bodies warmed up for the task ahead with every man fighting his own battle in his own mind. Then we heard the instructors call out, "Airborne. Got to go. Airborne!"

There were a couple of overweight guys in the ranks; after about three miles, we heard them fall out and hit the ground. We knew it when we heard their steel helmets hit the asphalt with a clang. We continued on with our run. I was feeling very good about myself because with five jumps I would be a PARATROOPER. My right knee was hurting, and the pain was severe, but I never missed a step. I had come this far, and I would die rather than turn back. So I began limping and running and dragging. I sang to myself all the way, "Got to go, Airborne, got to go, all the way. AIRBORNE!!!!"

Just up ahead we could see the finish line. Our spirits picked up; we had made the run and passed the course. It was a tremendous accomplishment in our lives. The next day we worked through everyday training for the last time and ran a few miles. Trucks came by to carry us to the airport. Upon our arrival, we found two parachutes laid out for our first two jumps. The date was June 27, 1961. We got into our harnesses and clipped on our reserve parachutes. Our instructors checked us thoroughly, and we entered the aircraft.

It was my first airplane ride and the first time I had been close to an aircraft. The plane was a C-130 Hercules, and I was seated with five other jumpers on the right side of the aircraft. The left and right side doors were open, and a BIG jump master stood in the middle between the two doors holding onto the cable that ran up and down both sides of the plane. We had to hook onto that cable with the static line which would jerk open our parachutes.

Our plane took off, circled the drop zone (a huge open area), and two other instructors started checking us out for the last time. The webbing on our chutes was pulled so tightly we were humped over and could hardly breathe. Then came the command, "Outboard stand up" (that was us, five at each door on either side of the aircraft). "Hook up, check static lines, shuffle to the door." (Now we knew what the Airborne shuffle was.)

Everyone has a number in jump school, and mine was 338. We were to jump one at a time. There were two lights in the plane by each door. The red light, already on, meant prepare to jump; but when the green light came on, we had to jump. We were cruising about two thousand feet above ground when I heard the jump-master call out the land marks below: "Illinois Avenue (seconds went by), 41-A, Stand in the door 338." I took up the position, eyes straight ahead, knees slightly bent, hands on either side of the door, And then I heard the simple little word that sends adrenaline throughout your body, "GO!"

Into the wild blue yonder I went. I was a para-trooper at last. No one could call me a leg ever again. The blast from the props hit us like a tornado, my feet went up, and I was parallel to the plane. As I counted 1000, 2000, 3000, 4000 and opened my eyes, I heard others who had found they were alive too. We floated on down to mother earth, all of us thinking, "That truck probably will not be there to pick us up."

I served three years in the 101st. I learned there are two things that stand out on all paratroopers: their boots shine like glass, as do the wings on their chests. They all also have a very short haircut. To some men, becoming part of a unit as special as the Airborne is like a religion. However, not everyone can accomplish or live with the danger that they love.

In those days, being in an Airborne unit meant you had to deploy anywhere in the world in a matter of hours. It also meant you had to be on alert twenty-four hours a day. Therefore, if your company was on first alert, it meant you had to stay in the barracks waiting for that mission to anywhere in the world.

Taking a bunch of GIS and locking them up for weeks was like a prison sentence. So if you were on first alert, the mess hall, the day room, or your bunk was about as far as you could go because you were on alert. We fought each other, we drank anything we could get, and we hated being locked up. The cloud did have a silver lining though. When our Battle Group Alert was over, we usually had a three or four day pass - Clarksville, Hopkinsville, and Nashville. They all knew when we had come to town. We had fights, disagreements, and partied a lot. We worked hard, too, all of us knew why we had become paratroopers.

I had always wanted to see Germany, so I considered that trip a vacation. I went on a number of maneuvers where the 101st encountered the 82nd Airborne. We trained with a number of branches of the service. I can say now, "If you want to go Airborne, go for it if you have the guts and you are ready to die for your country!"

January 12, 1964, was a cold day although the sun was shining. I remember it well, for it was the last day of my three years in service for my country. I went to the orderly room after breakfast, received a month's pay and my left-over leave pay. With about $300 in my pocket, I drove my '55 Chevy to Nashville, Tennessee.

Forty years ago I was a paratrooper, and I will never forget the training, the hard work, the danger, pride and satisfaction, and down-right love for "338

Stand in the door, GO." It took years to readjust to civilian life, but I have never regretted the many experiences and lessons learned that will stay with me forever.

Back to Civies

I had a party planned at Diamon & Leitha Donegan's. I had known them for two and a half years, and I called them Mom and Pop. . Their son-in-law, Stair Lancaster, and I were buddies in the same company at Campbell. He was a good paratrooper and a good friend.

We got to know each other on my cherry jump, which was my first company jump. You jump five times to wear the wings of a paratrooper, and Stair, sitting beside me, asked, "Are you a cherry jumper?" Well, that did it! I was fed up with all the insults, wise cracks, and indications that I was not accepted yet. So we fought right there in the aircraft in full harness as I was getting ready to make my first night jump. I climbed him, and he was three times as large as I was. The green light came on, and we hit the silk. Upon touching the ground, we fought until we were bloody and tired. So we sat down in the middle of that 1000 acre field called a drop zone and compromised. But he was the one who said, "Do you want to go to Nashville tonight and get plastered?" I had planned to go to South Carolina, but he persisted.

Pop met us at Eight and Broad in Nashville. I met Melba Donegan – soon to be Mrs. Stair Lancaster. We three did a lot of living together all through the years. Melba, an only child, loved me like the brother she never had. That first weekend Pop gave us his fast Pontiac station wagon, and we were off to Memphis to meet Stair's parents.

We left Nashville with empty pockets and a basket full of fried chicken on that slow road to Memphis. The chicken lasted only a short time. There was no interstate to Memphis in 1961. Melba met her future in-laws, and we had a glorious time traveling to and from Memphis. Melba, Stair, and I were to spend many wonderful hours together. Our love for each other has survived since 1961. Stair had prostate cancer that took his life, and I spoke to him by phone on his death bed. His last words to me were, "I love you, Charlie." Indeed it was true love among the three of us.

Melba Donegan Lancaster Moore has some of the most wonderful relatives. During my three years in the service, I cannot express how her family accepted and loved me like I had never been loved before.

It was through the Donegans that I came to have a second adopted Tennessee family. I came to love Leitha's baby sister, Ruth, and her husband, Howard Jackson. Ruth was and still is a gourmet "country" cook, and Howard was an artistic director of the United Methodist Publishing House for 30 years. These two are talented individuals who love crafts, blacksmithing, silver working, and life in general. They have always had a gigantic love affair with the world and a curious anticipation of things to come.

I will always remember the Donegans, who accepted me with an unconditional love I so needed; they loved me for what I was, with no questions asked. Whenever I was in town I was welcome in their home anytime, day or night. I continued to visit them until their deaths in the 90's. Yet I still return to Nashville to see the Jacksons and, of course, Melba.

I was living in Nashville, staying with the Donegans, where this nice looking young lady walked to the bus stop every day. Needless to say, she caught my eye. Melba met her at the bus stop and arranged a blind date for us. It was a wild courtship, and in seven weeks Judy I were married in Ringold, Georgia, the same place Stair and Melba were married. The judge said the vows too fast to suit me; after asking him to slow down, we still did not feel as though we were married. So Judy and I went across the street to a Baptist church and asked the minister to remarry us. I guess he thought we were "touched," but we felt better about our vows.

There was something special about our relationship. Judy and I were both the oldest kids in our families and had great responsibilities on our shoulders at a very young age. We also had chores and responsibilities everyday of our young married lives, but marriage agreed with us. We loved each other and respected each other's space. We knew we had to work, and Judy was a very good manager of our funds. The week I met her I had bought a new '65 Ford Mustang. I was single then and thought I could pay for it. The way it turned out we both paid for the car. We were very happy and proud of the little blue car, and I washed and waxed it everyday.

Our weekends were spent driving to Shelbyville to visit her folks, but occasionally we drove to South Carolina to visit my family. Those were happy days.

I had not been married a year when I experienced a dull pain in the back of my neck. I found a good physician, and he referred me to a mental health center. I was so ignorant of my condition, which I later learned was a handicap, that I could not fathom what lay ahead for me. My illness began to make life miserable. During the first three years of our married life, I was extremely jealous of Judy and very overprotective. I imagined her having affairs. She changed her employment for more money and peace of mind, but I made sure she was scared to death of me. I still loved her deeply, and she was the only person I really trusted with my life at the time. Somehow we made it in spite of my weird behavior: strange mood swings and uncalled-for anxiety.

My depression was moderate, but later it became severe. After a doctor's visit, I was referred to the Dede Wallace Mental Health Center in Nashville. I did not have any idea what was involved. During this time, I worked with three huge electrical companies in Nashville, requiring extensive work with dangerous electrical equipment. Mr. Donegan got me the job, but it required my completing my high school education. During this time, I was enrolled in the Dede Wallace Center, finishing high school, and had started attending night classes at the University of Tennessee.

My life was both happy and miserable. We moved from place to place, looking for a satisfying place for me to work to satisfy a mind that was going in circles. During those days, people did not notice my abnormal behavior because it would come and go. I was either in or out of a good or bad mood. What really confused them was the mean look I had on my face. Judy called it the "mean teen" look. I was suspicious of every living thing, but I learned to trust her, and I trusted her with my innermost thoughts and truly loved her.

I did rather well while attending classes at U.T. night school, but I could never read and comprehend what I was reading. I had a chemical imbalance in my brain. That means an electrical impulse in the form of a thought could not get through its natural path; therefore, most of the time my thoughts were incomplete. Since a thought is an electrical impulse from one point in the brain to the other, if it does not complete the circuit, you do not get the thought or message through. Believe me, it is very frustrating, especially when you do not know what is going on in your brain or your body. So, I could not read and comprehend although I loved to write. I do not like to read very much to this day because my mind has learned it is not a very successful behavior for me. My diagnosis!

The Mental Health Center in Nashville, which helped me understand my behavior, and my college courses in psychology went hand in hand. If you can imagine taking each behavior you have in your repertoire and analyzing it and changing it one at a time, then you would know what I have done for the last forty years. Always working to improve and learn new and better behavior has been a life's work for me. For example, I was in group therapy for a number of years. One evening we were working with someone on a particular behavior. I kept interrupting, asking questions, running my mouth when I should have been listening and concerned with someone else's pouring his heart out to the group. A therapist stopped everything. She said, "Charles, you are like a #X#X#X# mosquito buzzing around this room. You have no insight into what is going on. You are just running your mouth for attention. Shut up!" I had never been so dumbfounded in all my life. She was so right, and I owe that woman so much that I could never repay. She did her job that evening and showed me that I have to sometimes apply this to my life, but it hasn't been easy. I still have to get my two cents in, even if I have to yell.

This is the way behavior can be changed in the right environment with the right people in charge. It may scare some people to be put in that situation, but that was a drastic measure for a drastic situation. I was a guinea pig, but I learned a great, great lesson that I could not have learned anywhere else except in a clinical situation.

My particular group in Nashville was involved in helping with the research and the printing of a book called *Interpersonal Relationships*, by Dr. William Fitts of the Dede Wallace Center. We all helped; therefore, our first names were added to the cover of the book. We learned communication skills from Dr. Fitts. Four of us sat in a circle, with each of us assigned a skill. One person had to communicate a short message to the person who would receive the message. Another person had to observe the transmitter, and the other had to clarify the message. In the right situation, you will find out very fast if you are a transmitter or a person who just receives messages.

Although the normal person can use all four skills easily, it takes practice for someone to be good in all four areas. For those of us who lack this skill, just to be aware of what is happening in any given conversation is a joy. Group situations allow opportunity to change any kind of behavior. In groups, you can experiment with different types of behavior that you can learn to use outside the group or in what I call "real life." A good therapy group, like one-on-one counseling, helps prepare you for treatment. No one wants you to do it by yourself, and everybody wants to help you get through this time in your life. I was steered to psychotherapy because I had a tremendous amount of nervous tension in the back of my neck, which was really the beginning of my many years of hard work just to stay alive.

Back to the Greens

I stumbled around going from job to job, never being satisfied, until one day when I was having lunch with my boss at an electrical construction company. I told him I was looking for a job in the golf business but had not been able to break into the golf business in Tennessee. He just happened to know the right person, and I was hired by the professional at a very exclusive golf club.

I had done every job on a golf course before entering the service, and I was hired to do it at this club. I loved the people there and their families, for it was a thrill to work for the best. I would never have left there had I not become ill. I worked there a few years and made a good reputation for myself. I pride myself on being a man of integrity. When I tell someone I will do something, I do it. I do not lie, and I am always honest. This has been the secret to my success then and now. I do not fudge on any of these traits.

The professional at the club taught me many things, yet I could have learned more had I not been confused and ill. He was respected, and he taught me respect for him and myself; I was as proud of him as he was proud of me. He told everyone I was the best, and I was because I saved him thousands of dollars; therefore, I paid my way and did a great service for him.

My duties there consisted of being in complete charge of the electric cars, working in the golf shop, and keeping up the driving range. I was allowed to play eighteen holes of golf on Thursday afternoon. It was a wonderful job, and I loved it as much as I loved my wife and new son.

The hours were long, and I had very little time off. If your family was not golf crazy, working at a club would not work out for you. It is a tough life working for the public. You meet some wonderful people and some not so wonderful. The large private clubs, which are every professional's dream, are the ones to shoot for. I learned from the beginning that some people like you, some hate you, and others do not know how to take you or what to do with you. This has proven to be the truth in my life.

I have been around golf since 1950. Even though the P.G.A. has made great progress for the golf professional, the club professional sometimes has very little help. At least he has insurance and scholarships for the young golfer who may become a professional some day. But it has become apparent that you have to have a college degree in something just to qualify or get the chance to work in the business. The club professional in the middle of Nowhereville is the guy trying to scratch out a living for his wife and himself. Even those days are gone, for the clubs now get the golf cart rental fees and the green fees. The members also go to the city to buy their clubs, balls, and gloves. The only thing a club professional can sell is a package of tees and the balls he fishes out of the pond after hours. Where does that put the tournament player? He has the spotlight as always - the hero! Where is the golf professional who has a small club? The only thing he has is a small salary, yet love for the game.

I left and took a job at two different clubs in the next two years. I failed at both of them because I was young, inexperienced, and the clubs did not have the revenue to pay a professional. I always went in as a professional and a greens superintendent.

I continued in the golf business in Nashville until '71 or '72. I took the PGA exam, passed, and was waiting on my card when I made the decision to move to Atlanta to get closer home. It would have been a good move had I not been ill; my problems were constantly there, coming and going day in and day out. Two or three good days, then deep depression and anxiety.

I was running out of options. The one thing in the back of my mind was buying a home. I would not have a prefab home either; it had to be a good investment. I could not raise the money to do that in Nashville. I made good money in the golf business, but I could not get ahead, so I sold my car and bought a clunker. I still could not get a down-payment on a house. I was in Atlanta, and after a short time I was dismissed from my job - my very first dismissal. They gave me two weeks pay, and I went to South Carolina and home.

On the Move Again

Everything I had accumulated lay on my mom and dad's front porch. I was disgusted, for I knew Judy was humiliated and hurt. I looked for a job for months, just doing anything, but could not make connections. At last I gave up, loaded up, and returned to Tennessee. We always had money to move and rent for awhile, and I knew I could work in Nashville. We rented a small apartment that backed up to a creek and a railroad track. I was so depressed and ashamed, but Judy followed me and never complained. She was never one to say, "I told you so."

I bought some hand tools and went to work as an electrician. We rewired government housing projects. Each morning we had to enter the attics, and we came down as black as the coal dust in every attic. It was like that for months. I got rid of the clunker of a car and bought a big Impala for its size and room. I financed it, and, in the back of my mind, I was planning another move to South

Carolina. I knew it was the only place I could put a roof over our heads that would be ours. I was transferred to another job and put money in the bank. Then when I asked the owner of an electric company in my old hometown for a job, he said, "Come on down."

With money in my pocket and a loaded down trailer, I returned to South Carolina to make it in my home. I went to work, but I still had the same problems. I could not get along with people. There were only rare cases when I did get along. Later, I found I was paranoid on top of all my other problems. I thought someone was against me or trying to hurt me.

To my surprise, my employer sent me to work at a steam generating electric plant that was being built on the Penny Royal Road. It was harder at first than the attic coal dust of Tennessee. The boss's brother taught me how he wanted the job done at the site. The area was part pine thicket and swamp, and the deer loved the area. All the timber and undergrowth had been cleared away, and it was like a desert. The first day was terrible, for the temperature was in the nineties. We entered a huge ditch in mud and water. Our equipment was a grinder powered by a generator for sanding the glaze off the steel pilon and a five gallon bucket to dip the water out of the working area. There were two laborers who dug the mud and sand away from the base of each pilon. My job was to weld a piece of bare 3/0 stranded copper wire to each pilon. I had 2,499 to go. The mud and water had to be dipped out of the welding area so that the copper would stick to the pilon when welded. The steel had to be clean to make it stick. I will never forget the first day and the heat and sweat and bugs. The Nashville housing attics would be welcome to me that day. The job did get drier and the work easier, and time slowed down a bit. I was building a network underground of copper and steel for the grounding system of a huge electrical steam generator which would supply power for towns and factories. A twelve-foot thick concrete pad would sit on these steel pilons. Months went by, and I was the only electrician on the job site. Then, too, I was the only non-union man on the job. I tried to help out by getting temporary power to everyone I could help out.

I worked for six months digging in the summer heat in that swamp. The colored guy in charge of the laborers let me drink from their water keg, or I never would have made it. I did most of the work alone; it was better that way. The pay was low, and we stayed with my brother Jerry Lee. Judy and I slept on a mattress with springs poking out for a few months. I was not finished at the generating plant, and I returned to stay with my mom and dad for awhile. At this time we had found a small, three bedroom brick house on Longwood Lane, Conway, South Carolina. We fought the realtor for six months, and with the help of the G.I. Bill, we got our home, but not without a fight.

My wife and son and I had slept in some awful situations, but Judy had never had to work; she took care of our son. We moved into our new house on my birthday with a glorious inch of snow on the ground. We went home and had a roof over our heads. Judy lay down the law. She said, "Mister, this is the end of the line. You go anywhere you want to, but I will be right here waiting." I left the plant and went to work at the beach on hotels and motels. They were simple to wire, and the pay was better. I got mad at the company I was working for and went to the north end of the beach where a huge Hilton Hotel job was underway. There I met Henry. He was in charge and hired anybody that would show up for work. I liked Henry and did not mind working for him, but my real trouble was coming to a head. Henry let us work day or night and as long as we wanted, which was the worst thing for me to do. My condition got worse. After ten or eleven months there, I really had problems. The paranoia, the mood swings, the schizophrenia, and the depression were so bad I could not sleep. I was not resting, and I cried all the way to work. I pushed myself and pushed myself, for Judy was not working. I knew I had to make the house payment and put food on the table.

My problems got worse, for there were a lot of Masons on the job. Many were from the north and of many different trades. It was a treat for them to come to the beach for a few weeks or months. Some of the trades allowed them to bring their families, work on the job, and play afterwards. My condition worsened. I was sure the Masons were after me for not joining their ranks.

One day some young men were painting on a swinging scaffold which somehow broke or slipped, killing one of the men. One hung on for dear life while the other fell over seven floors through a glass canopy. They took me to show me where he fell, and I knew they were after me, too. I went home that evening and bought a pint of liquor. I tried to drink it and get some sleep, but it was impossible. I lay on a concrete floor and would doze off only to wake right up. Alcohol did not help. The next morning I went to work–half asleep–but I went, and I cried.

I had grown up in Screven Baptist Church of Georgetown, SC, and soon after Judy and I were married, I found out she was no Baptist. She never asked, ordered, or implied that I should worship at the Church of Christ, but I accompanied her anyway. The first time I went to church with Judy I met a man shaking hands at the front entrance. Later I asked Judy if he was a politician and what he was running for. She laughed. I never dreamed I would be doing the same greeting at the entrance of the Myrtle Beach Church of Christ after many years.

I became a member of Myrtle Beach Church of Christ in 1973, and someone told me a Christian could not call anyone master but Jesus Christ. "God is my master" was on my mind heavily, and, too, the Masons were after me. I went through a process of elimination in my mind. If I did this, then I could do that or make another choice.

When I got to work one morning, a huge crane was lifting a huge wooden platform. I stood right under it and called out, "God is my master!" I would not succumb to Masonry. I wrote on the back of the crane, "God is my master" in white letters. Months later, it was still there. I wrote the same on a door nearby, and Henry showed up. I was whimpering, and I walked to the beach with him by my side. We sat down, and he told me to let it out, but it did not help. He said, "Charles, I lost my dog last year, and I cried like you are doing now. Do not be ashamed." I knew I had to get home, so I missed my first day of work that year. That, too, was another goal I failed to reach, for I knew I had to stay in one place or I would not have a job. I had to stay, but I lost in the end.

I went to the church, and our minister, A.B. Carroll, called Judy. I followed her home, but it was not over by a long shot. That same evening I started packing a bag and told Judy I was going to Nashville to get some help. She knew I would not get far, so she and Charles came with me. It was almost dark when I decided to turn into a small hospital in Mullins, South Carolina, and see a doctor there. I went in and talked to a doctor, and, lo and behold, he had a Masonic ring on. I gave in. "Do what you will, for I cannot run any farther."

He looked me over and told me I had suffered a heat stroke from being in the tobacco fields. He said, "I am sending you to a Veterans Hospital in

Charleston." He told me not to drive myself home but to go home and to the hospital the next day. It upset Judy because she could not see to drive at night; but bless her heart, she got us home. I went to sleep, but early the next morning, my brother and his wife took me to Charleston's VA Hospital. I hated to go in there, and I was barely awake. I just knew I would lose my home, my wife, and my son. All that I had strived for was at stake.

When Push Comes to Shove

They admitted me, in spite of my protest, and Judy told them to keep me until I was well; they sure kept me. They put me to bed that morning, and I slept until 6:00 a.m. the next morning. They administered Stalazene, and I began to come around. I ate food for the first time in weeks. Although there were troubled times ahead, I began to realize where I was. I could not be released or even go home without Judy's consent. I started pleading for the first time in my life.

Some of the young doctors played ping pong in the day room at lunch. I found my doctor and asked him to let me go home. He said, "Stay longer and we will talk." Thinking about all I had at stake, I got down on my knees and begged him to let me go home. No deal! He took me by the arm and into my ward where he talked to me. He said, "Charles, you are just like a man with a heart attack. It takes time for your mind to heal." I had to accept that for then.

The next day I was hearing voices. I wandered into the day room where I found a TV and a pool table. There was a blind man there at the table (veteran or not, I never knew). He wanted to play pool. I talked to him and helped him play a game of pool. He loved that, and we became friends. Later that evening, I thought someone said I could go home. I was hearing voices again. I got very mad because they would not let me go, and I took a pool queue and hit the table with it, destroying the cloth on the table and the pool queue stick. The next day they moved the pool table to another room, and I was still in the VA.

Newcomers to the ward, like me, were confined to the day room. We took our meals there and lived there. Next door was the alcoholics' ward. Sometimes we mingled, but not often. At night, sometimes, we had live entertainment. I even got up and sang with the church groups. When the lights were turned out, I sat down by the night light and read my Bible and prayed. I prayed for Judy and Charles and our little home. I called her collect and frequently wrote to her. I still have the letters.

The members at the Myrtle Beach Church of Christ were wonderful. The old Impala carburetor had a gas leak. So a gentleman in the parts department on the air base donated the carburetor, and our men put it on for Judy to drive. They put food on the table and helped Judy get to worship services. We also went on food stamps. There was no income, but God saved our little house and made a way for Judy to come to see me. We may have had $300.00 in savings when I was admitted. Judy was fighting a battle at home with Charles, who had tried to ride the tailgate of a truck and fell off and hurt his shoulder.

I was still on a high dosage of Stelazene and still confined to the day room. I was there about a week when a fight broke out. Some guy had hit a man in a wheel chair in the face with a ping pong paddle. That stirred up things for awhile. Also, there was a red light in the office area that kept going off. I never knew why, but it looked just like a fire truck light.

One evening I was going to turn in early, and there was another guy in the room. He said, "Do you want to have sex?"

I said "Whaatt? Get away from me, you idiot."

He had something in his hand and said, "Take a whiff of this." He pushed it right into my face, and I saw all kinds of colors most of the night.

Time went on, and I adjusted the best way I could. There was a small inverted sitting area with a phone just off the mail hallway. Some guys stayed there all the time, listening to the radio and requesting songs. There was one song that was very popular at the time. All I knew was that I was not even on the way to recovery, and one song was played over and over, which was "Nothing from Nothing Leaves Nothing." Somehow I related to that, and it really made me feel worse, for the music played relentlessly, over and over, day and night.

In a matter of days I was sent to roll bandages, which I hated to do. I sat there awhile, and some of the men would take advantage of whatever situation was available. However, the most wonderful Florence Nightingale nurse always protected us from the others. There was another night nurse in charge from 11:00 p.m. until 7:00 a.m. who sat and talked to me. She pointed out the Citadel and other sites and rushed me off to bed. I can never forget Alice Fordham. She would lock those guys up that came in full of booze and screaming at the top of their voices. She was tough and a good nurse.

There was a certain secretary working the desk during the week, and all the male patients found her to be very beautiful, to say the least. I loved her and everyone on the ward loved her.

I met a nice guy among the patients. He was Airborne like me, and he was well-versed in the martial arts. Nobody fooled with him, but we hit it off. At nights we walked up and down the hall out of sheer boredom. Oh, how boring it was there! He would go to a contact he had and get cartons of milk. We would put them in the ice machine and drink cold milk until we went to sleep.

I smoked then, and we walked and smoked every evening. He was an excellent pool player, and few could beat him at the game. There were other games played there. When the evening shift, which consisted of a male and a female nurse, finished their paperwork, they played a game with us. We walked and walked, and they would throw small balls of paper on the floor to see which one of us would pick the paper up first. Were we bored or what?

I have always been a person of little patience, but those days in the hospital taught me patience. I had to be rehabilitated, and a lady whose name was Ms. Serwin had the task. Shortly after getting settled in, I had to attend her class. She gave me a 5"x 5" little tray to fill with very small pieces of porcelain. I had to glue each tiny piece to the little tray. When the tray was filled, grout was put around the open area, and you had a piece to sit hot pots and pans on at home. I hated that with a passion. I hated it even when I only had one space in the middle left to finish; so, we chose an acorn for the center and grouted the thing and let it dry. Once dried, you just wiped off the excess. I hated every minute of it, although Judy would fight you for the thing. She loved it although she never knew how hard nor how long it took me to accomplish the task.

Pain Becomes Progress

That was the beginning of returning to a sane mind. As I progressed, I did other things, and Ms. Serwin was so patient with me. I had another favorite in the class – a Mason volunteer! The gentleman was smaller than me. He was in his eighties and worked with us all the time. He had silvery gray hair and wore bifocals. I never would have dreamed in a thousand years that I would be working with a Mason during my recovery. We had fun, just the two of us, and I laughed for the first time in many, many months. He was a wonderful man. I will never forget him and his kindness.

You cannot imagine the trauma and shock that the separation from your loved ones causes when you enter a mental ward. I learned a valuable lesson during this time in my life. Therapy situations, groups and individuals, provide safety when you need it the most. While the outside world is rough and tough, hospitals are a very protective environment. We all need a place to heal that offers a free and relaxed atmosphere that is safe and wholesome at the same time. It is a haven we must have if we are to change behavior. What a relief it is to have that security. I spent sixty-seven days in the Charleston VA hospital on 5-B North. I thank God everyday for the Veterans Hospital and the love they have shown me. Some people just show up for work at the VA, but others are dedicated to helping the vet. I can never repay them for all they have done for me. I hear others griping impatiently, and I sit quietly, thinking, "Where would we be without the VA?" A lot of us would be gone and forgotten, and still others, who survived, would be sleeping in a box on the street if we did not have the VA.

There are many success stories involving mental health. I recall the case of a young man who was admitted to the hospital. I never knew his problem although I knew his wife ran off and left him and his kids. The state took his children, and I do not think he ever saw them again. After I returned home, I saw him, apparently in good health, with another lady to whom he seemed happily engaged.

Another case that I remember vividly from my hospital stay was a young man suffering from deep depression. We were confined at the hospital together. He told me he was really depressed, so he bought a fifth and went to a vacant lot where he found a good spot under a tree. He drank his liquor and cut both wrists, only to be found and rushed to the hospital. He lived to tell me, and I pray he found the right drug or chemical to give him a new life and happiness. You will never know what is going on in a person's mind until you walk a mile in his shoes.

Still yet, there was a case where a young man tried the easy way out with a shot gun. He put the gun to his chest and tried to do the job; the shot gun slipped and he mutilated his shoulder with shotgun pellets. Unless he found a miracle in some kind of surgery, his arm and shoulder are completely useless to him. You can read about these experiences in a number of books and magazines, but I witnessed these cases with my own eyes. When people have thoughts like this, they need to go and get some help. If they miss or fail to take their lives, they are in worse trouble than when they started out in the beginning.

One man, an expert in his trade, always drank a lot. One day he went home and put a pistol to his head and pulled the trigger. The son-of-a-gun lived and was an invalid the rest of his life. He cost his entire family all they had to meet his expenses and keep a man alive who was unsuccessful at taking his own life.

On Higher Ground

There is no real and wonderful cure for the problems of this world. You can stay in a therapeutic situation all you want or need to, but there is a point when you must help yourself. I met a woman one day who gave me the best advice I have ever had from a pure stranger. I told her about my problems, and she gave me the answer in two words: "Get religion."

I became a Christian on April 4, 1973. At the time I did not know what it meant to be a Christian, nor did I know how many years of attendance, fellowshipping, studying the word of God, and praying were ahead of me before I became aware of the love I had for God. I tackled religion just like I tackled mental illness. Full speed ahead and ignore the torpedoes! The torpedoes are the devil that is always waiting for us to make those wrong decisions that we spend the rest of our lives trying to repair. We can do anything we want with our lives, but just as God gave Adam and Eve a choice in the garden, he still gives us a choice. Somewhere along the line, we have to come to grips with our innermost mind. The only way to do that is through the love of Jesus Christ and God our Heavenly Father.

Studying my own behavior, taking medication, participating in many group sessions, surviving in and out of psychic wards, and long years in the church are what have kept me alive. Oh yes, killing myself was on the top of my list for a number of years. I am happy to say I have never actually tried, but that did not stop me from the thoughts that are as real as any way of dying you can dream up. The scriptures tell us life is like a puff of smoke compared to eternity in heaven.

You cannot do it alone when you are as manic depressive as I am. However, I have in some ways overcome some impossible odds with the help of others and Jesus Christ. Some may laugh at the mention of heavenly help or divine intervention. However, when you face the idea of death because of a breakdown, looking down the barrel of a gun could not be any more frightening; for I have been there and done that, too. When your mind tells you you are about to die, it is as real as smelling the gun powder. When you go through a process of elimination of the events that are going to kill you, then that old rugged cross and the blessed Jesus who died for us is right out front where you may touch it. It is there, and it is real.

It took a long time for me to become a solid Christian. For many years I was not able to be in crowds, could not stand loud noise, and just wanted to be in a quiet, secure environment. It was to me like having a huge ulcer in my stomach all the time with no control. I trembled, ran from many healthy situations, and avoided most all of the fun times of my son's growing up. Life was miserable for me and for my family also.

Support from your family is a must during mental illness. I always had trust in Judy and my son. They both made many sacrifices so that we could be together and take care of each other. Judy was a wonderful Christian who stayed in church, always keeping our son Charles with her. Judy is responsible for our family's being in church every Sunday. In the twenty-eight years we were together, she rarely said "I love you," although she proved it to me and to Charles every day.

My life with Judy was a wonderful life. We respected each other's feelings and each other's territory. I will never forget our very first apartment after our honeymoon. We lived upstairs from a landlady who loved to talk, but we always had other things on our mind. The very first weekend after we moved in we went to work on our new home. Everything had to be spotless, and I agreed to it. I, too, learned how to keep house as well as she did in the years I had to stay at home.

The day after we were married, Judy's mother told me right out, "Judy is a good woman; do not forget it." She was right as I found out through the years. Judy combined the best of both South Carolina cooking and Tennessee cooking. She could whip up a meal in just a few minutes. She kept the home finances perfect within a few pennies. She was a hard worker, and to me she was the perfect woman.

Our first years were full of love, and, as the years passed, we found strength and more love for each other. However, I smoked constantly for many years, and after being in the hospital, I doubled the amount I smoked. I cannot help but believe that my second-hand smoke had a lot to do with Judy's lung cancer.

When the doctor told us she had terminal lung cancer, we were speechless. It was a sad winter day. She took the chemo and radiation, and we paid the price. During the many years I had to stay at home, she worked for a nursing home. Professional that she was, Judy put in a half day's work the day she passed away. That evening after she came home from work, she passed away in my arms.

Judy raised a perfect son who took his marriage vows seriously and gave us four grandkids she never saw. Never a day goes by that I do not think about her, and I often dream about her. She was the greatest thing that ever happened to me. Many women would have walked off and left me, but we both meant our vows, "Till death do us part."

Judy sat down and wrote beautiful letters to her mother, brother, and sister before her passing. I have the one she wrote to me. It is filled with the love she had for her family and me.

"To Charlie: It's been a great twenty-eight years. We sure had our tough times, but God was good to us and helped us muddle through until we got it right, don't you think? I guess most couples would not have stayed together, given some of the problems we had, but I believe it made us stronger. We were blessed far more than we ever expected and got a perfect son and now a beautiful daughter-in-law to round out our little family. You have been my oldest and best friend for so long, and I have depended on you for so much more than you realize. I couldn't have made it without you. I hate to leave you so much, but if I must, you remain faithful so we can meet again forever. I love you, Judy."

The years have gone by fast, and I have been alone for ten years now. I could have gone out and just married someone, but I am still hanging on for a good Christian to worship with me and be a good grandmother.

I receive treatment from the VA in my area and can always return to Waccamaw Center. That is a comfort for a person who has been fighting mental illness for more than forty years. I have come a long way and have received a lot of help. Where would I and others like me be had we not known about or taken advantage of the tremendous advances in the mental health field? Dede Wallace Center and the Waccamaw Center for Mental Health were the centers that kept me alive. Some of the doctors, psychiatrists, and therapists at these centers have been the reason for my success. Although it took years to get where I am with myself today, I have a life these people gave me through their help, hard work, caring, and love for me and mankind. My fight has been hard. I will never again be able to hold down a job. But if I can help my neighbors, especially my church members at the Georgetown Church of Christ, hold my granddaughter on my knee, and piddle in my garage, I think my heart will be in shape to be with Judy again in the Promised Land.

The End

A Message From the Author

My intent has been to cover some important points about mental disorders, mine in particular.

This is for those who suffer from mental disorders, and I encourage them to heed this advice from someone who has been there. The following is a letter to a friend I met just once. This is what I told him and his wife:

I am manic-depressive bi-polar and have fought a battle for 40 years. Determined that I would be cured some day, I would never give in to it. Nevertheless, there is no cure for a chemical imbalance of your mind or brain. Yet there are drugs today that will make you think you are cured if you stay on medication. You may have a better quality of life although the problem or problems will still be there. How you maneuver in your environment, circle, or family situation depends on YOU. You must find the answer, and the answer is there. If you look and work hard enough, you will find that you do have the answers to your problems.

Therapy, whether best in a hospital or as an outpatient at a mental health center, is essential for a start. This is to improve your mental health and solve some of the problems that seem impossible to live with. You have to recognize there is a problem and want to change your behavior and your life by getting it back into a perspective that is real and manageable for both you and your family. Begin the process by taking stock of yourself. Write down the highest times or points in your life and just the opposite, the lowest points, too. Don't forget what happened in the middle of your life from the beginning of your memory to the present.

Take a good look at what you have done, where you have been, and what is going on in your life right now. This can give you enough information to decide what you want to do and where you want to go with your life. Where you are headed at present is your choice. You can accomplish these goals by setting up short and long term goals. If you are sincere and truthful with yourself, you can be on your way to better mental health. Take stock of yourself, your situation, and your feelings.

Learn what you feel, and determine if your feelings are controlling you or your life.

Feelings and decision making do not mix in most cases. It takes facts to make some decisions, and feelings of the heart do not enter the picture. Be aware that some feelings, like the grandson or granddaughter on you knee, are uncontrollable feelings but they are the ones that you can just plain enjoy. The point is to make reasonable decisions for you and the family, for they depend on you.

If you can look at yourself in a mirror or see yourself in a video, would you be pleased, displeased, or satisfied? I would settle for satisfied if I knew I had done my best in life. Would you be pleased with where you are in life at the present time? What would you change about yourself or your situation?

I received treatment from the Veterans Administration and, later, at mental health facilities. The help is there if you are interested in helping yourself and others around you. I mentioned in the first volume what it is really like to have a complete mental breakdown. It is very difficult to live through this alone, but, if you have family, it is closely related to alcohol or drug abuse. I mean it affects the entire world around you and especially your family. I cannot make you well, nor can anyone else make you well. However, in the last 40 years new medications and practices have been discovered that greatly improve life for those of us who have abnormal behavior. It is not just taking a pill; therapy can make you aware of what is around you and how you can live in this world. THERE IS HOPE!

SOME THINGS NEVER CHANGE

I am not just talking about the thoughts a woman has when she admires a man, nor am I talking about a man when he admires a woman, but the thoughts parents might have when they look at their sixteen-year-old daughter or son. This is a feeling and a behavior we might all experience in our lifetime as we raise our children. Is it sexual? Is it bad? If it is, then most of the women and men in this world are in trouble. It is a very natural feeling or thought to admire a child or teenager we have nourished from birth. However, we still feel guilty for such feelings because we feel it is not natural. Hogwash! A feeling is a feeling is a feeling like a thought is a thought. Thank God we have feelings and thoughts. When a person feels bad about these feelings, then we are having feelings about feelings, but this can influence how you feel about your children, husband, wife or the human race in general.

In my lifetime, I've had to take each aspect of my personal behavior and each feeling I could identify in my repertoire and virtually put them under a microscope and change that behavior or feeling. I tried to improve each one and use it in my everyday life. Is that impossible? No, it is not, for everyone has the same feelings; but few people can recognize or analyze their own behavior or another person's behavior. It is not that difficult. I repeat, everyone has the same feelings, but what happens when a person has a behavior that goes to the extreme? The same person who has sexual feelings for a child and actually fondles or goes to the extreme and has sex with a child is mentally ill; he or she needs help desperately. It is terrible, is it not? However, that is real life, and that is the reason mental health facilities and care are so very important to our society today. We also have laws that enable us to lock up people who cannot control their behavior. Sadly enough, some people are mentally ill and refuse to get help. Mental help is available in this country, and although some people are forced to participate in some sort of program, others never get help nor will they take advantage of the help that is available. How do you tell a person their behavior is unacceptable? How do we say, "You are crazy"? How do we treat people in our own families when we know they have mental problems? There is something you and I and everyone else needs to know and accept. We are all mentally ill to some extent in some area of our behavior. You can call or label it anything, but we are not all perfectly sane. It has been said that both Patton and Winston Churchill were manic depressive, believe it or not. If one of these heroes had fondled a child or let it be known he had some weird thoughts or weird sexual practices, would they have locked them up? Probably not, and they would not be found on someone's couch spilling their guts out. In our recent past, people with obvious mental or emotional problems were hidden in the closet and shunned by society.

My own personal opinion is that a person is mentally ill all of his life; but the degree and the time in his life is important. I do not think a person can be sure of a mental disorder. When mental health professionals can cure the chemical imbalance in my brain, ensure the transmission of my messages to make a complete thought, and cure the paranoia which has prohibited my holding down a job my entire life, then I will change my thoughts. The world is saying "We can cure you," but I say as long as I have to take medication and have no control over the paranoia and cannot function like a normal person, then I am not cured. Today I have Prozac, Xyprexa, and a very important drug for my condition, Divalproex, that controls a lot of my behavior. However, there are some behaviors I have never been able to control.

THERAPY, PILLS, & RELIGION

This is the combination that has really saved my life. My diagnosis had religious overtones. I never knew what they meant, but I thought I was about to die. Weeks went by before I realized I was to live after the breakdown. I grew up going to church as a youngster, but I fell away from it all during the service to my country. I was baptized into the Lord's church in 1973 where I have remained to this day. I am very deeply religious. I have studied the scriptures and very rarely missed a service. I participate in the church service when I am called upon. You might call this testimony. My dear wife led me to the church before I had my breakdown.

Naturally, I called on the Lord for help, and I guess they call it religious overtones.

The point I make is this: I could not make it then, nor can I make it now without God's help. My life, my wife, and my son's family revolve around the church. No man, woman, or child need fear death when they have G od in their lives. The reward is heaven and life everlasting with God in heaven if we do as he commands us to do. Mainly worship Him.

The Bible is the most sought-after book in the entire world. On the black market one may cost as much as $300, $400, or even $1000. While some of us in the United States of America own a number of Bibles, we rarely read them. Yet there are those who would risk everything to own a Bible.

It is an amazing book with 2930 people or characters. The first book covers 2280 years of life on earth. The entire Old Treatment covers 4,100 years of history and life before Christ. We live by the New Testament today, and the scriptures have an answer for every problem man encounters in life. It is a road map, a guide for every step of our life's journey. It covers marriage, divorce, love, hate, and what to do in all phases of life. It tells who will judge us all and when and by what law.

Man cannot add to nor take away God's law; for the word of God will last forever, and man cannot influence or change a single word of the scripture. No matter what you focus on in this life or the afterlife, God has provided an answer in the scriptures. God is in control of this world, and man's wickedness is closing in on him as usual. God gives us a choice just as he gave Adam and Eve a choice.

DEFINITIONS OF TERMS:

Manic depressive behavior or Manic-depressive Bi-polar illness is just what it means: behavior that is a combination of two behaviors that are just the opposite of one another. A person may be very high and excited for a period of time, and then depression takes over. They are opposite in nature. It is not hard to diagnose because the symptoms will be there sooner or later. The problem comes in diagnosing the disease when a patient may not be to the extreme in either direction at a given time. If you are having a mood swing and you are in the high phase of it, you can stay awake for days and nights. You can work relentlessly for hours, feeling no fatigue. You may talk or chatter all the time, smoke more, and never stop until you collapse. You may be unable to sleep or relax and just cannot slow down. Then the mood might change slowly into depression. At this point, your mood is very low and your self esteem hits rock bottom. You can feel so low and down in the pits that you think of taking your own life. You have to decide whether to live or die. You may call on God, a bottle of strong drink, or maybe pity from someone you love, but your mood is still down very low and you feel worthless. In that case, you must seek help right away. In my case, I have taken Lithium for these mood swings and Lith-I-bid and now Divalproex or Depakote, which is anti manic. There are a number of anti-depressants on the market today to help fight depression. The drug I use is Prozac or Fluoxetine. It seems to be the best to use in my case for depression. In my case, it takes a combination of drugs to fight bi-polar manic depression.

It is not hard to find these drugs in books at your local pharmacy. The drug and its history, symptoms, and side affects are right in your local library. Nevertheless, it takes a medical doctor's prescription to use drugs, for these drugs are not sold over the counter. Never think you can doctor yourself. It takes a professional who has studied and is involved with a certain patient's illness everyday to recognize the symptoms of abnormal behavior.

Paranoid Schizophrenia is what my diagnosis has been for many years. Whether or not the doctors agree, it certainly has been true for me. I cannot hold a job until this day due to delusions of persecution. Paranoia has been my downfall in my attempts to excel in any kind of work or any kind of relationship with people other than family and, most of the time, the church membership. I was able to trust my wife even though I have always been extremely jealous. This is behavior I had to learn about myself and learn how to live with, to some degree. I have never been able to control that part of me, but I understand what is happening to me with people and can cut some happenings off at the pass, so to speak. To be paranoid is like the coward who dies a thousand deaths, yet people like me put up the front that frightens most people away. One therapist called it the tough-guy image. In the Airborne, you had to believe that or die. At the time it seemed appropriate since I have always been willing to die for my country and Almighty God.

Since my first hospital visit of 68 days, I have taken many types of medications. These are some that I have taken in the last 40 years: Thorazine was my first medication; then I moved on to Stelazine for a long time, then Sinequan, Navine, Trilafon, Mellaril. The latest have been Divalproex, Prozac, Risperidone, and Hydroxyzine. Risperidone helps the nerve endings and the receptors to get the message through to a complete thought. One major problem I had was not getting the complete thought through my mind or brain. It turned into repetitious thought. Or the thoughts would start but could not make it completely thought. It is very discouraging to try carrying on a conversation when you can't complete it. Nevertheless, understanding what is happening to your thought process is half the battle. The last drug I have used very successfully is Hydroxyzine. It is used as an anti-anxiety agent and is a very good sleeping agent. It works for me both ways, and I could get very little rest without it. The last drug I will mention is one that did a good job for me for quite some time: Zyprexa or Olanzapine works on the chemicals and receptors of the brain. It is a good drug if managed correctly.

Drugs are a must if you have a disease similar to mine. Therapy is equally important because you have to learn your feelings and your thoughts and what is happening to you at any given time. I call it tuning in to your mind and your body! This is so very important to the treatment, for if you can convey to others where you are and what is going on in your mind and body and in your brain, then you can help yourself.

I have a degree in "practical" Mental Health: it has been my life long desire to overcome my handicap. If there is a winning side I have made it. Remember, there is no sure fire cure, but, with hard work and persistence, you can have a better life. I could scare you to death with terminology and experience. Most people are still unaware of what I am talking about. The mentally ill do not have to be locked up except in very rare cases. I take my hat off to those who have loved me and worked with me and are always trying to help others in mental health situations. Today a person does not have to be put away, but be careful what you say and where you say it. The public has not caught up with science.

Hope, Love, & Help
Within the Church

was baptized for the remission of my sins before I was admitted to the Charleston V.A. hospital for 68 days. I was like a choir boy among some of the patients. Many of them hated me for my belief and thought I was weird. At the time, I was weak and helpless. I have always stood my ground as a man, but the past years have found me humble and weak. I had to learn how to blend humility with strength and, at the same time, stand my ground. This is as important to a man as having children is to a woman. Men are made to be head of the household. Eph. 5: 21-25 reads, "Women, obey your husbands, and husbands, love your wives as Christ loved the church and gave himself for it." Some folks interpret that differently today, but God does not. God's laws are the same today as they were when he put them into effect. If you compromise that, you will not compromise divorce. Man did not make the laws of God. Yet people want to change God's words. The point is that we have no hope if there is no God. I know there are those who have laughed at me and God's word.

Yet I am strong once again, humble yet strong. God took me away from the golf profession I loved. Either God or Satan put me flat on my back and out of commission for years and years. My wife was taken away from me, and my son and I still grieve today for her love. Hope is what keeps us going, for Judy asked us to be faithful and meet her in heaven someday. Hope sometimes is all we can have or afford. God and his word give me comfort every hour of the day. Do I sin? YES! Everyday. I do not mean to, and, by his grace, God forgives me. That is where my hope and my faith in God come in. I know God loves me, and I know, as Abraham, Moses, and Job knew, there is life after death. They knew it before Christ, the son of God, died on the cross of Calvary for the sins of all mankind. Hope, so be it!

I am 63 years of age and full of love. Thank God I have love for God and all those around me: young folks, little folks, old folks, babies, men, and women alike thrill me everyday with a smile, a hug, or a handshake. There was a time when I was so full of hate I just wanted to kill. I chose the Airborne to take the hate out of my life. I hated the world and God for a long time, trying to be lean and mean. I did not want to do this His way. He loved me enough to spare my life for a purpose: one part was to find the peace and love for Him, and the other part was to serve Him. He chose me and loves me and now, like Paul, I am his prisoner. I love him with all my heart and strive to serve Him. I pray for the day I can sit at His feet and worship Him.

The church has always been a home to me, and you must remember how those of the congregation took care of my wife and son when I was unable to help myself. I had no idea they would go out of their way to help someone like me. Why should they? Because we are Christians and God does take care of his people. Try to imagine how hard I worked to get the little house we were living in when I was struck down. I was the first in the family to own a home. God gives us material things, but we have to make an effort also. God answers prayer, always. However, it will be His answer and His gift in His time. We may not like His decision, but He is God, and His wisdom supercedes any of man's decisions, wishes, or prayers. He is head of the universe. So be it!

What is my status right now with mental illness and with the church? I know who I am, where I have been, and where I am going; and I am satisfied. That is good mental health. Not too many people can be satisfied with themselves in this day in time. The folks closest to this would be Christians. Why! The materialistic things in life are our downfall. A better job, a bigger paycheck, a larger house, a fancier neighborhood, a bigger car, a country club membership. While it is alright to be wealthy, we worship material things rather than God. One cannot have peace of mind if the idols of today control us. We cannot have anything without God's allowing us to have it. There will be no RV following our hearse on the last ride we take, and we will not have one penny in our hand when we stand before God on judgement day. The Word of God and Jesus Christ shall judge us all, for before him every knee will bend and every tongue will confess his sins.

Where am I right now? I am comfortable, not hungry or thirsty, happy, content to be alive, and feeling good in general. I have to be aware of this all the time in order to function. We do this naturally most of the time although I had to learn every behavior, feeling, and need my body required. Is it hard? No! Each of us has these basic needs in order to function, but when one gets out of line, a feeling, a basic need, or a rise or fall in temperature can signal the brain for an adjustment. It may be a sexual feeling that arouses our senses. Whatever the case, our behavior may be affected in some way. Life is not hard, for it is appointed that each of us will die and face the judgement. What we do from birth to death is our life, but our God gives us a choice.

Mentally, I can make it to my last days if I steer the course I am on today. Am I cured? No! But I have learned to cope with people and with life. I want to continue to serve God in the church when I can. I am not ashamed to say, "I love you." For I mean it when I say it. I have witnessed powerful men pray and humble themselves before God. Life is good! Amen!!

Thank you

I have always wanted the opportunity to thank those who helped me through life and through my mentally handicapped periods when my self-esteem was so very low:

Charley and Mable Lambert
All My Family
The Dede Wallace Center of Nashville, Tennessee
Waccamaw Center for Mental Health Horry
County, South Carolina
Ralph H. Johnson Medical Center 109 Bee Street
The Veterans Administration Hospital of
Charleston, South Carolina
The doctors who cared for me and all the nurses
(men and women)
The therapists who labored many hours
The Church of Christ who provided for my family.
and helped me for many years, loved me and met
my many needs as a Christian
God bless you all!

Order Form

To order additional copies, fill out this form and send it along with your check or money order to:

Charles Lambert

9589 Sullivan Dr, Inlet Estates

Murrells Inlet, SC 29576-7208

Cost per copy $15.00 plus $3.00 P&H.

Ship _____ copies of *Abnormal Behavior* to:

Name_____

Address:_____

City/State/Zip:_____

___ Check for signed copy

Please tell us how you found out about this book.

___ Friend   ___ Internet

___ Book Store   ___ Radio

___ Newspaper   ___ Magazine

___ Other _____